"In these piercingly honest poems occasioned by the death of his beloved wife, Sarah, S T Kimbrough, Jr., gives unguarded voice to his grief. This is not easy reading because these poems force us to face not only the death of those we love but our deaths. These are searing poems, but in a strange way they are beautiful."

—STANLEY HAUERWAS, Professor of Theology and Ethics, Divinity School, Durham, North Carolina

"In these 33 poems by S T Kimbrough, Jr., I found a depth of love, grief, passion and power that poetry alone can convey. My heart was melted and my resolve to live fully and die well was strengthened. The journey of life and death—grief and loss—is artfully presented. This little volume will bless and benefit many."

—THOMAS R. ALBIN, Director of Spiritual Formation and Congregational Life, The Upper Room Ministries, Nashville, Tennessee

"Kimbrough writes of the reality of the death of his wife in poems that express grief with emotion, tears, and faith. His acknowledgement of the enduring love of God and of his own love for his wife is based on the grace given by God in times of hurt, grief and loss. His poems also tell of the fact that even within 'grief there is hope,' comfort and assurance of God's presence."

—JOYCE D. SOHL, Laywomen-in-Residence, Scarritt Bennett Center, Nashville, Tennessee

"I am moved by Kimbrough's ability to translate the many feelings that go with death and loss into words that he is now sharing with others. I am sure these poems will be a comfort to those who read them. They also model for others the power of writing to access inner strength and wisdom during a time of grieving."

—PEGGY J. KINNEY, Hospice Bereavement Counselor, Duke Hospice Bereavement Services, Duke Home Care and Hospice

Of Death and Grief

Of Death and Grief

Poems for Healing and Renewal

S T Kimbrough, Jr.

Foreword by
J. Richard Watson

RESOURCE *Publications* · Eugene, Oregon

OF DEATH AND GRIEF
Poems for Healing and Renewal

Resource Publications
An Imprint of Wipf and Stock Publishers
199 W. 8th Ave., Suite 3
Eugene, OR 97401

www.wipfandstock.com

PAPERBACK ISBN: 978-1-5326-4372-9
HARDCOVER ISBN: 978-1-5326-4373-6
EBOOK ISBN: 978-1-5326-4374-3

Dedication

The author expresses deepest appreciation to his deceased wife of fifty-nine years, Sarah Ann Robinson Kimbrough, who in life and in death enriched his life with the fullness of beauty, art, and love, which his words can never adequately describe. This little volume is dedicated to her loving memory.

For Sarah

Though eight score years her life did last,
its final ending came too fast!

She laid her lovely body down
with pain and suffering as a crown.

Mercy with grace abridged her years,
and took her from the vale of tears.

Her gifts of kindness, love, and art
live on for ever in the heart.

God, her soul's eternal Lover,
round her let your angels hover.

S T Kimbrough, Jr.

Contents

Foreword

When S T Kimbrough Jr.'s wife Sarah died after a happy marriage of fifty-nine years, he sought, as all who have lost loved ones do, to try to come to terms with what had happened. He did so by writing the following poems. They record the emotions of a strong man almost overcome by grief, holding on to whatever comfort he can find. Sometimes that comfort came by putting his emotions into verse, trying to find words that would express his grief, the dreadful lying awake in the night, alone (that lying awake is memorably explored here in "Sleeplessness, Grief's Torturous Friend"). Sometimes it came from the consciousness of something else, a mysterious feeling that somehow the response to death is related to love, and the memory of that love is all-consuming, even in the face of death. Memory, as Kimbrough writes in "Grief's Redemption," is like a dove, the gentlest of birds:

> Grieve on, brave heart, for in grief
> there is hope, there is belief
> that memory like a dove
> alights on the heart with love.

The pain of parting is terrible; the memory of the moment of farewell is so painful, a moment that is captured here in the restrained simplicity of

> It was fifty-nine years ago
> that I saw her for the first time.
> A month ago I saw her for the last time
> and kissed her lips for the last time as she died.

Memory and pain and love come together. As Emily Dickinson put it:

Parting is all we know of heaven,
And all we need of hell.

The feeling of disaster and loss at the end of a beautiful relationship will never go away. And yet there is gratitude for what has been, for the mystery of the last days, for the care received against the inevitable process of dying, and for the presence in the room of something other-worldly in the wonder of the final precious days and hours. And then comes the reality. One of these poems records the attempts of others to console, seen against the misery of turning the key in the front door. When they say "How are you," they ought to know how hard it is, each day to enter an empty house, but

The simple words, "You're in my thoughts"
suffice beyond all measure.

These poems indicate something that we all know, but often lack the courage to explore, the intimate relationship between love and grief: that the more one loves, the more one grieves when that love is brought to an end by death. And yet, as these poems show, love continues to exist, in the continued presence of the beloved in the mind and the heart. As one of these poems says:

Give thanks for love, for being—
for life, feeling, and seeing.

"For being." The phrase is simple, yet exactly right. Just "being" is a gift that we need to remember to give thanks for. And somehow, that love continues through all the accidents of life, and through the final moment of death. It is not easy to say how this happens. We may believe in heaven, and that we shall meet again on another shore and in a greater light, or we may not. But whether or not we have such a belief, there is a sense that love continues beyond the last embrace, or the last kiss on the forehead. Death is a farewell, but one in which we carry with us the knowledge that parting is in some ways impossible. It is like the end of Sarah Doudney's beautiful hymn, "Sleep on belovèd, sleep, and take thy rest": "Good night! Good night! Good night!" Doudney's note reminds us that the early Christians were accustomed to bid their dying friends "Good night"; and that hymn carries with it the thought that has been a part of the encounter with death for more than a thousand years: *Requiescat in Pace*, "Rest in Peace." And yet it also has the simplicity of a familiar action, the last words spoken before going to sleep. The ordinary words of daily life are used here to say a last farewell: it is part of the way in which life and death, love and grief, are inextricably and mysteriously combined.

These poems are a moving personal record of a precious relationship. But they are also addressed to all those who are striving to come to terms with loss and bereavement. This little book will be to those who mourn, a comfort to the brave hearts who grieve at a time that we all have to face at some point in our lives.

J. Richard Watson[1]
Durham, UK

---

1. J. Richard Watson is Emeritus Professor of English, University of Durham, UK, and a long-time friend of Dr. S T Kimbrough, Jr.

Preface

The Story Behind the Poems

THIS LITTLE BOOK OF poems reveals how I have dealt with the grief that accompanied the death of my wife, Sarah, the love of my life for fifty-nine years. The poems are a conversation with myself on the journey through the grieving process, which perhaps has no end. Yes, they are permeated with a deep faith that there is more to life than merely living and dying. At the same time, they are honest responses to how painful it is to lose one's life partner. We had a wonderful life together, which took me through three collegiate degrees, including a Ph.D., all of which I could never have accomplished without her support, and took her also through three diplomas, R.N., B.A., and M.A. She bore four wonderful sons who more than anything taught us how to live and the value of loving one another passionately.

When I published books, her read-through of a manuscript was essential, and she was often my best critic. When I sang opera in Europe, where we lived for many years, at a final dress rehearsal before an opening night she would often sit in the theater and take notes, which were often invaluable in shaping my performance.

She studied art and became an exquisite artist, developing a style of relief painting, one might call three-dimensional, that was captivating to the viewer. She was, however, a very self-effacing painter, never feeling that she was finished. She thought there was always more to do to improve what she had created. When we returned to America, we lived by the sea for many years and, hence, sailing and sea motifs became characteristic of many of her works. She was very clear that she was not painting to show off what she had done, rather the most important thing was that she been given the gift to create. If someone liked her paintings, fine. If not, that was also just fine.

At the age of seventy-seven she was diagnosed with Parkinson's disease. She continued painting that year but in the following year she no longer had the stamina to continue for she had always stood as she painted.

Over the next eight years the debilitation of the disease took away the motor skills of her lower extremities, and finally the body became too weak to sustain life, and the love of my life died.

We lost one of our sons in a tragic automobile accident a few years before her death, and we both thought this was the worst emotional challenge we would ever face. We were not there in the moment of death to be of comfort. The absence and coldness of his death was almost unbearable for us. O yes, we are people of faith, but faith, as comforting as it may be, does not take away the sudden pain of the instantaneous loss of a child. Faith can help one through such tragedy, but there is no simple answer to grief.

The death of my wife was completely different from the death of our son. During the last nine years of life her health gradually declined because of the Parkinson's disease. I was her sole caregiver through it all, and my grief over her death was doubly intensified by the loss of my daily caring for her. The fact that I could no longer do for her what I had done through those last years was extremely painful and filled with intense anguish. There was a major difference, however, from the death of our son: I was there with her to the very end. I could hold her in my arms, tell her I loved her, kiss and caress her beautiful face. It is so different when you can be there with someone who is dying and you can share an embrace.

Yes, there were many tense moments in those last years when it was difficult to know what to do and how to respond when medications evoked responses uncommon to one's behavior. It was a tremendous blessing that my wife's mind remained very sound to the end. The greatest blessing for both of us was our intense love for one another and for our children, and our unswerving faith. We laughed and cried together, and in the last months when reading was tiring for her, I read poetry, Scripture, selections the Sunday edition of *The New York Times*, and from her favorite author, C. S. Lewis.

Another special blessing for Sarah was her friend Janice, a colleague and friend in the same art group for many years. What Janice did after we moved to another state some 500 miles away, where my wife could receive the kind of long-term care she would eventually need, was almost unthinkable. Almost twice every year Janice traveled to spend a week with Sarah. Janice would often draw and paint, and sometimes early on when Sarah was still strong enough a museum visit was a must. A month before Sarah died Janice was with her for one of her annual visits. There is no substitute for the comfort of a friend!

Some of the poems are autobiographical, and the very first one in free verse, "As If It Were Yesterday," is about the first time I met Sarah, our marriage, our life and love together, and her death.

The actual physical occurrence of death can be readily described by physicians, but its emotional and life effect on us is much more illusory. Without question, these poems are simply one person's response to death and grief. They provide no decisive answers on how to respond to either, but if one's open and honest response can help others address such challenges, so be it. However, I must be clear, when I wrote these poems, I did not write them with a view toward publishing them but to help me through the journey of grieving. A few grieving friends with whom I have shared them encouraged me to share them with others by putting them into print.

I know there are focus groups for grieving and positive steps one may take to assist the grieving process. I have read much valuable literature shared by hospice organizations and other groups for the grieving. My goal is not to provide steps for the grieving and healing, but rather through poetry to share the thoughts of the heart and mind as they grapple with death and grief.

I have learned through this very difficult process, which may never end completely, that love alone is the key to healing: love of the dying, love of self, love of others (family, friends, and perhaps someone one may not know), and love of God. There is no chronological order of these loves for they are all intermingled. Although the poems are organized in three sections: *Death and Dying, Grief and Grieving*, and *Love and Loving*, the persistent theme throughout is that only love in many forms is what sustains anyone facing death and grief.

S T Kimbrough, Jr.

As If It Were Yesterday

As if it were yesterday, I remember
the moment I waked with excruciating pain.
Immediately I pressed the call button.
What then happened was miraculous:
The most beautiful woman I had ever seen
appeared at my hospital bedside.
Her nurse's cap nestled on her flowing black hair,
and her deep, dark brown eyes were intoxicating.
She asked, "What may I do to help you?"
Totally enchanted I said, "Will you marry me?"
No doubt she thought I was delirious
from the surgery's anesthesia and resulting pain.
Ignoring what she must have thought was delirium,
she asked again, "How may I help you?"
I unhesitatingly repeated, "Will you marry me?"
With a smile she turned and departed
only to return relatively quickly with
medication to assist with my pain,
motivated no doubt by my persistent groaning.
Momentarily thereafter the pain was relieved
and I floated it seemed as if into oblivion
with visions of her wonderful beauty.
That was in January, and in November
of the same year we married.
She became my wife, mother of our sons,
lover, and care-giver of us all,
who traveled with us to the ends of the earth
to make a home in a foreign land.
It was fifty-nine years ago
that I saw her for the first time.
A month ago I saw her for the last time
and kissed her lips for the last time as she died.
There was not a wrinkle on her beautiful face
at eighty-five years of age! No, not one!

To me she was as beautiful at that moment
as she had been when "love at first sight"
overwhelmed every part of my being.
Grieve though I may for my remaining years,
"love at first sight" was also "love at last sight,"
which is as it should be.

Prologue

God, Whose Love Revives the Soul

God, whose love revives the soul,
make my grief-torn spirit whole.
Take away the gloom of night,
turn my darkness into light.

Teach me ever the new way
love's enrichment to display.
Transform sadness into joy
through the gift of love's employ.

Anguish transform into peace
through the hope of love's increase.
In the midst of grief and pain
let me sing a love-refrain.

Love in life and death God's will;
Christ the pattern for the skill
love to practice and to learn,
ever with its fire to burn.

Section 1

Death and Dying

1. The Power of Death?

Death makes my inmost nature quake
    not for fear that it shall come,
rather knowing that it shall take
    life's calmness and peace from some.
The powerful expense of death,
    whose cost can never be known,
takes life in one expiring breath,
    be one young or fully grown.

Faint before the power of death
    or find in it divine grace?
Can there be grace in one's last breath?
    Perhaps, if love leaves its trace.
Love removes from death its power,
    known or unknown or revealed.
Death cannot conquer in its hour:
    to its grasp love will not yield.

From Palestine of ages past,
    resounds the authentic claim
that love's power will death outlast,
    indeed, love is life's sole aim.
So be it in death there is life
    as claimed Jesus and St. Paul:
love-graced life will subdue death's strife
    and every human-made wall!

2. Death and Life

With utter stillness comes death
as mortals take their last breath.
Death is life's eternal chain;
death is grace for those in pain.
Death for many means relief
but for others often grief.
Death for some's a shibboleth—
unanticipated death!
Its finality and shock,
an emotional gridlock.
For the living, there is life
filled with comfort, rage, and strife.
Some are empty or alone;
others want for sins to atone.
Death leaves everything behind:
love, possessions, all in kind.
One may weep and one may mourn
or give thanks the dead were born.
For the time they dwelled on earth,
long or short, treasure their worth.
Deepest love is worth the time,
for the faithful, is sublime.
Give thanks for love, for being—
for life, feeling, and seeing.

3. The Anguish of Death

Worn down by emptiness of heart
    when sleep no longer is a friend,
I cannot bear that we're apart,
    but death, my love, I cannot mend.
The chasm, the vast gulf between,
    a darkness we've not known before,
leaves you, my love, in life serene
    and me where there is peace no more.

There is no peace without you near,
    without your cheeks to kiss, caress.
My longing for you chafes like fear—
    my anguish builds to wild excess.
Our lives long we have lived by faith
    that love eternal binds our souls,
that love divine creates no wraith
    but living, vibrant human wholes.

I have not lost this faith we claimed
    the moment we became as one,
but death has left my heart so maimed;
    reality I cannot shun!
I pray anew, our faith to own:
    in life, in death divinely met,
that in my heart your love is shown
    in ways I never can forget.

4. Death Absent and Near

Absent death orchestrates the mind
    and heart with strains of agony
that leave one's spirit lost, confined
    to gruff grieving's savagery.

A child is lost in raging war,
    How did he/she die, you want to know.
You're told, "He/she died. There's nothing more."
    "Nothing more!" the worst kind of foe!

A foe of all one wants to ask,
    "Did he/she die in dire pain, alone?"
Is "Nothing more!" a shameful mask
    of truth no one can ever own?

Quite similar is instant death
    not in some distant, unknown land
which takes a loved one's final breath
    and you're not there to hold a hand.

The emptiness one can't ascribe—
    except to one soul vanished, gone!
One cannot easily describe
    the sense there will be no new dawn.

Different is death when one is there
    to speak one's heart and then to feel
the beating heart with tender care—
    moments that death can never steal.

But some of us are left on earth
    after death instant or death calm.
Parents mourn those whom they gave birth,
    a spouse is left with little balm.

Still life goes on, and those who live
　　must find the reason not to think
that they have nothing left to give,
　　grief's depth to which they dare not sink.

God did not create senseless life
　　but with the purpose love to show
that every moment can run rife
　　with love that heals—this we can know!

5. Where Is the Long-Awaited Calm?

Where is the long-awaited calm
    that follows death's disrupting storm?
Is this a myth of senseless balm,
    a cultured tale, a storied form?

Yes, all is quiet, all is still,
    while turmoil roils within my soul,
and solitude can never fill
    the void of one who made me whole.

Drained of my strength from floods of tears
    and torturous, heart-troubling thought,
can I escape the horrid fears
    with which my mind and soul are fraught?

And dare I trust the prophet's truth:
    "Wait on the Lord," strength will renew—
old words that echo from my youth.
    Dare I believe that they are true?

Shall my vocation be to wait
    upon the Lord for strength renewed?
Yes, wait, wait lest it be too late
    with peace and calm to be imbued.

Can I be sure this will take place—
    the post-death, long-awaited calm?
My weakened, troubled soul by grace
    shall sing again with joy a psalm?

This only comes to those who wait:
    a gift when waiting has been tried.
Yes, wait! wait! lest it be my fate
    to live when I've already died.

6. Death's Holy Grail

The memory of that dreaded hour
    when death snatches life from the soul
brings grief to consume and devour—
    emotion beyond all control.
If sorrow enters and remains,
    on a dark precipice one stands
which plunges to unending pains
    beyond the reach of human hands.

Although one is confused, and void
    and emptiness floods sense and sight,
be not by conscious grief destroyed
    or life becomes a desperate plight.
There is a source of human care
    transcending loss and bleakest night;
in still and quiet it is there,
    the solace of assuring light.

Divine introspection awaits:
    the patient most surely will find
that reflection in prayer creates
    peace and clarity of the mind.
Look inward for the constant calm
    that reassures death can't prevail;
for body, mind, and soul the balm,
    this is the lasting Holy Grail.

7. Till Death Us Do Part

Till death us do part, easy words
    to the young who will make this vow.
Liltingly comes the phrase in thirds,
    "I love you" eternally, now.
If kept the vow promises pain,
    though preceded by life with joy,
one cannot foresee all life's strain,
    destiny can be a decoy.

The vow makes no promise of time
    to fulfill the dreams of the heart.
Though life may seem more than sublime,
    swiftly the time will come to part.
Two lovers must cherish each day
    as though every hour were the end,
without fear and daring to say,
    "I'm blessed with you my life to spend!"

8. Grace-Filled Death

I shall not now retire to grieve,
    though death has left an empty space;
transfixed with sorrow I'll not live
    or life is destined without grace.

Acquainted I am with sadness
    and wept I have within the vale
where death's throes rob one of gladness,
    but grace the heart will never fail.

Nor life, nor death can now disjoin
    the love that eternally binds;
and death itself cannot purloin
    the joy in love one always finds.

Yes, grief turns on its fatal course,
    one's spirit is forlorn, undone.
It arms as a resistless force
    and presses one all life to shun.

What can assuage and quiet grief?
    a crucial, vital human need.
In love, I shall find true relief—
    and be miraculously freed.

Yes, grace-filled death there is I know
    when suffering and pain are past,
and love subdues all grief to show
    anguish, despair need never last.

9. Embrace the Dying

Haunted by expiring pain
    till the soul and body part
tenderly your love sustain,
    hold the dying to your heart.

Trying though this be and hard,
    your embrace the dying need.
Love withheld will leave you scarred.
    Your embrace one must not plead!

Love endearing at death's door
    hinders grief's seductive force.
Pain on us it vents no more
    when love only is life's source.

Grief, death's partner, lurks each hour
    life and death to rob of worth.
Death is not an evil power,
    nature's course, as is our birth.

Every dying soul love needs
    as companion through the vale.
Faithful love most surely leads
    to life you'll love or bewail.

Love for the dying will show
    mercy's not smothered by grief.
Embrace the dying, you'll know
    love alone offers relief.

To every suffering heart,
    troubled and grieved by one's death,
the power of love will impart
    reason for life and for breath.

This love is yours and is mine
 Though mysterious its source—
indubitably divine—
 the world's most powerful force.

Section 2

Grief and Grieving

10. Grief Is but a Breath Away

Grief is but a breath away;
loved ones gasp, you're in its sway.
Slowly, swiftly it will come,
your soul's depth alone to plumb.

It does not respect your flight
from its fated depth and height:
Its chilling grasp, taut and cold,
its caustic power, brash and bold.

Yet, there's wisdom couched in grief,
rich in strength, in calm relief.
Think not selfishly of pain,
grief self-centered traps the sane.

It can injure thought and mind
till by grief life is defined.
Though all life is stilled by death,
still give thanks you yet draw breath.

Grief does not define the end
but becomes the moment's friend.
If your thoughts it does not reign,
its strong grasp is sure to wane.

Think not grief you should forget
rather know death is no threat.
Life and death the Maker's plan
in eternity's time span.

11. Grief

If grief cannot be turned to grace,
    there is no hope of gentleness;
If grief cannot be turned to hope,
    no dreams there are to cure illness.
If tears of grief are but disguise
    for angels' soothing elegance,
then grieving mortals must be wise
    to know each tear has relevance.

12. Grief's Redemption

This morning grief pierced my heart
as arrows flesh cleave apart.
Emptiness, no! I felt pain—
pain as if my soul were slain.
My love is lost forever!
The love, which naught could sever!
Drowned by a cascade of tears,
embraced by thoughts of our years;
suddenly I remember
that glorious November
when each of us said, "I do":
an eternal "I love you."
Grieve on, brave heart, for in grief
there is hope, there is belief
that memory like a dove
alights on the heart with love.

13. When Grief's Dark Shadows Fill the Heart

When grief's dark shadows fill the heart
    and anguish seems beyond control,
when love's strong fabric's torn apart
    and there is emptiness of soul,
in prayer look inward, you will find
the strength to calm an anguished mind.

Prayer lets in the angel of calm,
    brings peace to the riddle of strife;
it soothes like the shade of the palm,
    affirms beyond death there is life.
Look inward in prayer, you will learn
you must not with grief's torment burn.

God visits the mind through our prayer;
    divine visitation assures
that destiny's not always fair
    in spite of its human allures.
Look inward through prayer, there to seek
God's will when your spirit is weak.

The prayer reservoir of God's love,
    the source of divine human care,
awaits like the rain from above
    to shower with strength grief to bear.
Look inward in prayer, there's the source
of power for the length of life's course.

14. More Grief?

Will this day pass without more grief?
Its shadows give me no relief.
They cover me with darkness grim
till anguished thoughts grow yet more dim.
How this shall end I do not know.
If only a clear mind could show
a glimpse of future clarity,
there would not be disparity
between my thoughts and how I feel,
and my existence would seem real.

15. Grief and Questions

Why do people say, "How are you?"
    When they know you've lost your spouse?
Surely, they know it will jar you
    to enter an empty house.

The simple words, "You're in my thoughts"
    suffice beyond all measure.
When one's soul is writhing in knots,
    questions evoke displeasure.

There is no question you can ask
    of one in anguish and grief.
There is no grief that they can mask;
    no quick answer gives relief.

A hug, a kiss, a calm embrace,
    a quiet and simple prayer,
will leave your love's most caring trace,
    the lasting sign you were there.

16. The Answer to Grief

When shall all my grief be spent
    and all my suffering end?
Comes a day without lament
    for my loved one and my friend?

With the slightest touch of pain
    how can tears be wiped away?
Love was swept from earth again,
    and I remain here to stay.

I languish with deep desire
    and yearning to touch her hand.
Did joy forever expire?
    Was this what life for us planned?

Death's anguish is so severe
    when trapped by grief and by woe.
Love's closeness from year to year
    is absent, vanished! I know!

Will all my suffering cease?
    Will all of my grief be past?
Can I find enduring peace,
    an inner calm that will last?

One moment I now reflect
    that my pain cannot compare
with the dastardly effect
    of her sickness and her care.

From her sweet and tender lip
    never heard I a complaint.
Regardless of its tight grip
    she bore illness as a saint.

So, this mountain load of care
(I think has weighed me down)
is indeed a mental snare,
for death she wore as a crown.

Yes, a crown for those who bear
the load of sickness and pain
with sweet demeanor, who share
a strong faith that does not wane.

Faith that life is so much more
than merely our life and death:
God lets humans love explore
instantly from their first breath.

Here is the answer to grief:
The gift of love to explore.
The foundation of belief:
God has more of love in store.

17. Sleeplessness, Grief's Torturous Friend

Sleeplessness, grief's torturous friend
    has me firmly in its hold.
Last night's waking was without end,
    a feeling of bitter cold.

There was no tossing, angry threat
    as quietly I lay there.
I did not break into a sweat;
    my thoughts were empty and bare.

And yet at times a flashing thought
    reminded me of my loss;
still in sleeplessness I was caught
    each hour full of waste and dross.

O yes, I know "Just let it go,"
    resounds a wise one's advice,
but death is such a heartbreak blow,
    emotionally a vice.

Still sleeplessness I will not mourn
    though wearied, tired I may be,
for it reminds me love was born
    between my lover and me.

Side by side many years we slept,
    without a thought of the time
when one would all alone be left
    without life's "reason or rhyme."

Not so, as death for one drew near
    we knew that reason and rhyme
had filled our lives from year to year,
    for love remained in its prime.

God gave us children, wondrous years,
    our lives were forever filled
with laughter, joy, anguish, and tears—
    on love, we learned life to build.

Perhaps these memories will ease
    my sleeplessness in the night.
Though my loss they may not appease,
    grief's burden they'll make more light.

18. A Prayer for the Grieving

Are we born to grieve and die,
trembling with the question, "Why"?

Grief that anguish does not spare,
turns my soul to God in prayer.

Within bounds of time and space
let my pain mature to grace.

Soothe my grief by patient love,
words as soft as sings the dove.

Sorrow, gloom be chased away
let the dark give way today.

Calm o'erwhelm my troubled breast;
sleeplessness transform to rest.

Let love all my grief control,
quiet peace o'erflow my soul.

Let not death's enduring smart
dominate my mourning heart.

With pain, death, and anguish nigh
humbly now for peace I cry.

Though my life seems dark and void,
let not grief be misemployed.

Let not all my grief be vain,
turning to imagined pain.

Teach me answers to my prayer
in myself have oft been there.

Teach me love alone secures
life against all would-be cures.

Help me grasp this simple truth
taught by loved ones in my youth.

19. Grief Is Ever on My Mind

Grief is ever on my mind,
my emotions lag behind.
Shall I grieve, and grieve, and grieve
self-resistant to forgive?

What in grief must I forgive—
the stark truth that I must live?
Shall I now grief deprecate,
life renewed appreciate?

In a solitary place
one can find the gift of grace.
Quiet finds the soul's release
and a long-forgotten peace.

Does this mean complete release
and that all one's troubles cease?
No, it means a wounded soul
can find love that makes one whole.

A sequestered wilderness
oft relieves the trial of stress;
there resisting every groan
one discovers love has grown.

With the gift to meditate
comes the gift to separate
selfish grief from honest care,
knowledge love is always there.

Faith, hope, love we learn these three
endure for ages, set us free.
Love is greatest of the three!
This is life's enduring plea!

20. Secret Grief

Secret grief does not lurk for show;
    it silently deceives one's heart.
Hid from oneself the threat may grow
    till faith and reason slowly part.

To cure the spirit's anguished mood
    from whence one's miseries may flow
what can constrain the heart to brood,
    if all one thinks upon is woe?

With grief's distraction, vision marred,
    one's heart of flesh may turn to stone,
unless one's thoughts become unbarred
    to punctuate, "You're not alone!"

'Tis then a barren soul may bloom
    with thoughts of others, flowers of grace;
and life's intention from the womb
    is then fulfilled in time and space.

Faith in an unseen God of grace
    survives alone in reason's view,
if "love of others" takes its place,
    center of all you think and do.

When neighbor love is at the heart
    of life and living day by day,
the unseen God becomes a part
    of faith and reason's guided way.

21. The Risk of Grief

The risk of grief—it shatters trust
    in others, self, in grace divine;
and grieving doubt is rarely just,
    it seldom will with love align.

The cause of my ongoing pain
    is sought in every soul disease,
yet death and grief it did ordain—
    no pale excuse can it appease.

My forfeited tranquility
    evokes the anguish of regret;
recovered through sincerity,
    I ask, "Can I my grief forget?"

The load of grief I have to bear
    would make my spirit faint away;
but grace responsible and care
    seek healing love without delay.

This all seems nebulous, complex,
    for grief, itself one can't define;
yet, all the senses it can vex,
    assure emotional decline.

Beyond myself I now must look
    to others and to grace divine;
then I'll know if the risk I took,
    renewed my trust by love's design.

By love's design, divine it be?
    No simple answer comes to mind,
for certainty's a mystery,
    yet, I'm assured God's love to find.

22. The Power of Grief?

Does grief come my soul to steal?
　　Can I grief and pain gainsay?
Death leaves me without appeal,
　　nothing can its grasp allay.

How then shall my soul prepare
　　when I'm sorely so undone
by the grief of snare on snare
　　long before my course is run?

Grief comes not in soft delays;
　　empty joy and painful woe
mark its path of anguished ways,
　　and love's hope prevent to grow.

Shall I doubt and trust no more?
　　Griefs transfixed and multiplied,
like cascading waters pour,
　　drowning me on every side!

"Stop," I say, "You shall not win,
　　though you would my soul subdue.
Never shall I faint, give in,
　　there are other powers than you!"

From these shall I draw my strength:
　　love and hope you cannot kill!
They will go to every length
　　to help the grieving heart be still!

23. Make Not of Grief an Idol

Make not of grief an idol;
   make not of it a shrine,
restrain, as with a bridle
   its torturous design.

Grief can bring restoration
   of what you feel within;
your spirit's inspiration
   can soon begin again.

But love in the equation
   of life and death must be,
or grief is but evasion
   of true humanity.

Love's presence is ensuring
   grief will not always last.
Love has an ageless mooring
   in life that is steadfast.

Love before and after death
   alone helps you survive.
Love is life's eternal breath;
   it's why you are alive.

24. Grief Comes and Goes

The maxim sure: grief comes and goes,
or long persists in lasting woes?

Time does not limit grief's sojourn;
it may depart and then return.

At daytime, nighttime, in one's sleep,
its visitation makes one weep.

Sad memories it may evoke
or joyous ones, as if one spoke.

Mourn not the grief of glad recall,
give thanks for blessings great or small.

Though sorrow is not always brief,
love whispers softly its relief:

"Think not one's soul it may possess!
To love, all powers acquiesce."

Do not think grief the end to be;
love's power reigns eternally.

25. Misdirected Grief

Grief sadly one's soul misdirects
    one's thoughts, emotions, all in one,
and steadily the mind infects
    with pity till life is undone.

Grief fosters a tormenting fear
    that life will never be the same,
and day by day more wounds appear,
    as witnesses of grief and blame.

Grief's cycle often can become
    a dreaded, bleak, dark destiny,
with swings of mood both drab and glum
    till life is an infirmity.

Will I let aggravated grief
    turn my own heart of flesh to stone?
Will it turn faith to unbelief?
    Will I not trust in the Unknown?

Should my soul void and naked be,
    vulnerable and without cause?
It needs new eyes of faith to see
    the course divine on which it draws.

God, grant me patience of new hope
    as mercy fills my hungry soul
with energy and strength to cope,
    with all there is to make me whole.

If grief should hasten to restrain
    the spirit, body, and the soul
with images of morbid pain,
    pray, let them take no mental toll.

Remove the soul-resisting bar,
   my desperate infirmity,
self-serving grief let leave no scar,
   and free me for eternity.

26. The Brighter Side of Grief

Deprived of all of reason's force,
grief marches forth on its own course.

By weighted woes of grief confined
there seems no exit for the mind.

Grief never let direct life's course,
lest days be filled with deep remorse.

Its stubborn bent to mourn is real,
but somehow it must help to heal.

The brighter side of grief I seek,
for not to mourn indeed is weak.

To love and not to mourn one's loss
covers the wound with mental gloss.

What pattern shall I keep in view?
To love, to die, to grieve, renew.

Thus, can I consecrate my pain
to love I gave and now regain.

Hour by hour, also day by day
love can the wounds of grief allay.

To every grieving, suffering heart
God can the power of love impart.

No longer then will grief confine,
its hold will soon become benign.

This brighter side of grief I see
can quell the storm of grief in me.

Section 3

Love and Loving

27. Love and Grief

So much alike are love and grief,
    though this comparison seems strange.
How can joy of one's heart-belief
    compare with radical heart-change?

Can weeping compare with laughter,
    elation with devastation,
loss with love forever after,
    one's kisses with love's cessation?

Both give us joy, both give us pain;
    their odd likenesses a puzzle.
Grief wills our loss and love our gain,
    grief to love's words is a muzzle.

We laugh, we cry, the body feels
    an inner alike sensation;
in love, in grief emotion reels
    with different expectation.

O! they can conquer, love and grief,
    be victors over heart and mind,
steal sanity like a sly thief,
    leave one to misery consigned!

Only when one foresees a life
    of welcoming to love and grief,
can one endure forthcoming strife—
    know love as life's lasting motif.

28. The Medicine of Love

To death's grave malice now I'm left
    and by its anguish I am torn;
of peace and joy I am bereft
    and mourn as one who is forlorn.

Shall I a hopeless mourner be?
    My spirit groans within, "How long?
Pray, help my soul's infirmity!
    In death is there both right and wrong?"

I thought to be to grief inured
    and out of death's dust to arise,
from all the pain that I've endured
    to sense a life that never dies.

For those who seek to hoard their grief
    there is but wretchedness and pain;
the respite from its load is brief,
    for earth and joy there's but disdain.

If there is healing for despair,
    and comfort here below, above,
help the unbearable to bear:
    it is the medicine of love.

29. Absence Makes the Heart Grow Fonder

"Absence makes the heart grow fonder,"
    so, the daily proverb goes;
yet at death one's left to ponder
    simple truth one rarely knows.

Fonder grows the heart most surely
    when the loved one is away;
death grasps absence quite securely—
    this is truth that's here to stay.

Can love grow when death has taken
    love's dear presence from one's eyes?
Though illusions will be shaken,
    love that's faithful never dies.

Can a broken heart grow fonder
    when a loved one is not there?
Only if one does not squander
    love that grief would oft ensnare.

30. Constancy

When waves touch gently on the shore
    and the horizon greets the sun,
the constant waves daily explore
    the shifting sand with each wave's run.

There is a patience in the sea
    awaiting neither life nor death;
its constancy can set one free—
    miracle of the Maker's breath.

The sea stops not when grief sets in;
    it roars or patiently it stills.
Its cycle then begins again
    with gentleness or raging thrills.

When sorrows start and then prevail,
    the sea stays on its constant course.
One may lament and grief bewail,
    the sea remains a steady force.

Learn from the sea indeed one may;
    it whispers to one's inmost soul
"Do not fall victim to grief's prey;
    life will go on from pole to pole."

The sea says, "Stop, collect your thoughts!
    You cannot change creation's course;
You choose not life and death by lots,
    gifts are they from a divine source."

The constancy of life's a must
    which from the ocean we can learn—
as sure as tides return, we trust:
    Love alone—life's constant concern.

31. Stronger Than Death

How weakened my heart
with my love to part.

I languish in vain
her love to sustain.

I once more confess
I am in distress,

for death took her life
and left me with strife.

What now can relieve?
I grieve and I grieve.

How hard to declare
the sorrow I bear.

How dreadful the cost
when love has been lost.

And now every hour
I feel the lost power.

Love's glorious grace
I saw in her face,

the rapturous height
of love's sheer delight.

And where am I now?
Where was it or how?

I do not yet know
how I can let go.

How shall I now move
to mercy and love?

Yet what could destroy
such innocent joy?

"Our love did not die!"
My heart speaks the cry!

In love and in death
love yields not one breath.

Its strength will endure,
eternally sure.

So in my despair
I now turn to prayer,

for love to sustain
in spite of my pain.

And all the day long
I pray for a song

of love to live by
and not to ask, Why?

32. The Eternal Art

An aching heart steals my sleep
   by day, by night, and at noon;
it broods, it yearns, makes me weep
   and turns my life to a swoon.

Would my inner vanished calm
   could invigorate anew
my crushed soul with Gilead's balm
   or fragrance of morning dew.

Can my heart sound love again
   when my love's rapture is gone?
When the one who once was twain
   wakes to singleness at dawn?

Forget not: Love is ageless!
   Can this lessen my despair?
My inner self now rages
   for my love's no longer there.

Forget not: Love is ageless,
   comes again the haunting cry.
This truth becomes contagious,
   though it does not answer, Why?

One moment of reflection
   of love shared from year to year
evokes the sure rejection
   that love died because of fear.

The fear death could take away
   all love's treasures from the heart
is doomed to fail if you say,
   "Love is the eternal art."

33. To Live Again

Can we grief's dark mood restrain
in the midst of loss and pain?

Grief can rule the stricken heart
and resist its rule to part.

Sorrow comes, the heart is rent
with no comfort in lament.

Tears we shed oft naught avail;
time and sense, we both bewail.

Death we in our bodies bear,
yet love's lasting place is there.

Hence, in death to love we turn;
there to live again we learn.

How, we ask, can this then be?
Live again, but by degree.

Step by step to live again,
love will make the pathway plain.

What can love our life afford?
Life by miracle restored!

Epilogue
God, Whose Love Revives the Soul

God, whose love revives the soul,
make my grief-torn spirit whole.
Take away the gloom of night,
turn my darkness into light.

Teach me ever the new way
love's enrichment to display.
Transform sadness into joy
through the gift of love's employ.

Anguish transform into peace
through the hope of love's increase.
In the midst of grief and pain
let me sing a love refrain.

Love in life and death God's will;
Christ the pattern for the skill
love to practice and to learn
ever with its fire to burn.

www.ingramcontent.com/pod-product-compliance
Lightning Source LLC
Chambersburg PA
CBHW070831100426
42813CB00003B/570